Write Colour

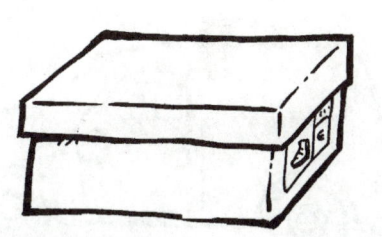

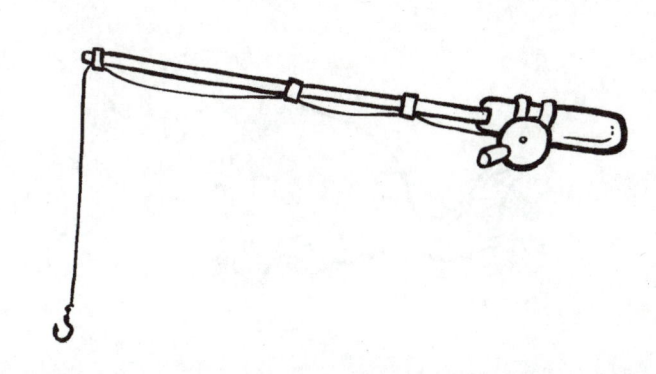

© Carol Doncaster and Joyce Sweeney 1995.
These pages may not be photocopied.

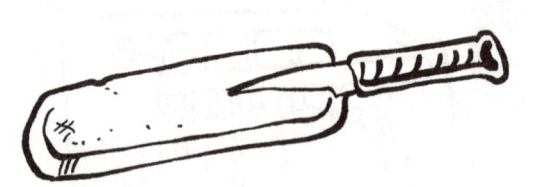

Write ☐   Colour ☐

© Carol Doncaster and Joyce Sweeney 1995.
These pages may not be photocopied.

3

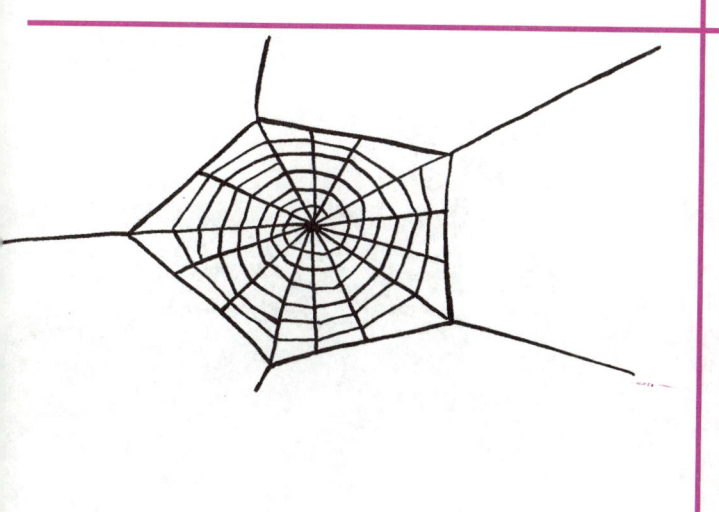

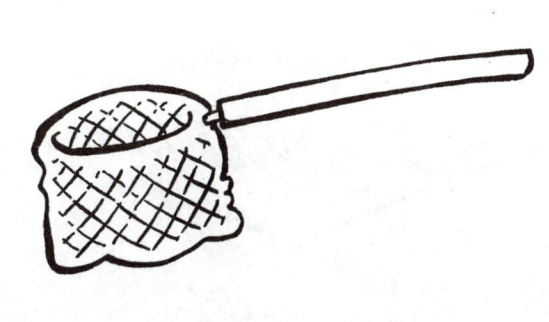

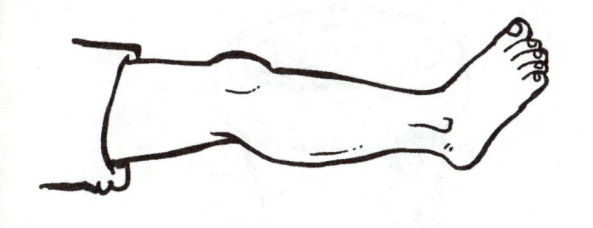

Write ☐   Colour ☐

....

....

....

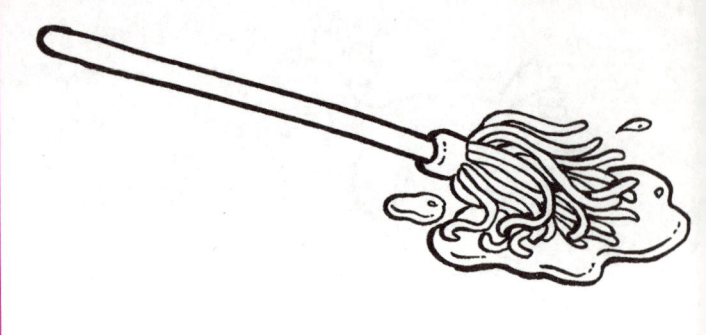

Write ☐ Colour ☐

....

....

....

....

....

....

© Carol Doncaster and Joyce Sweeney 1995.
These pages may not be photocopied.

Write ☐   Colour ☐

© Carol Doncaster and Joyce Sweeney 1995.
These pages may not be photocopied.

Write ☐   Colour ☐

© Carol Doncaster and Joyce Sweeney 1995.
These pages may not be photocopied.

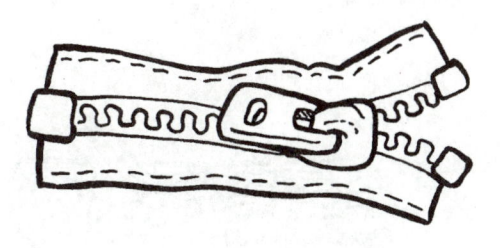

Write ☐   Colour ☐

8
© Carol Doncaster and Joyce Sweeney 1995.
These pages may not be photocopied.

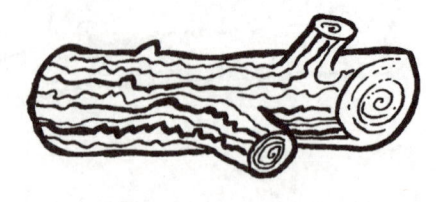

Write ☐   Colour ☐

....

....

....

Complete ☐ Copy ☐ Colour ☐

Jim is on the _____ .

....

A man is in the _____ .

....

© Carol Doncaster and Joyce Sweeney 1995.
These pages may not be photocopied.

Complete ☐   Copy ☐   Colour ☐

The _____ is on the pot.

....

The cat is in the _____.

....

© Carol Doncaster and Joyce Sweeney 1995.
These pages may not be photocopied.

Complete ☐   Copy ☐   Colour ☐

Jen is a fat _____.

....

Sam sits on the _____.

....

© Carol Doncaster and Joyce Sweeney 1995.
These pages may not be photocopied.

Complete ☐   Copy ☐   Colour ☐

Ted is in his _____.

....

The egg is in a _____.

....

© Carol Doncaster and Joyce Sweeney 1995.
These pages may not be photocopied.

13

Complete ☐   Copy ☐   Colour ☐

Pam has a big _____.

....

Mum has a _____ of pins.

....

Complete ☐   Copy ☐   Colour ☐

Jim has _____ mugs.

....

Ann can fix the _____.

....

© Carol Doncaster and Joyce Sweeney 1995.
These pages may not be photocopied.

15

Complete ☐   Copy ☐   Colour ☐

Jan and Rex can _____.

....

Rex is at the _____.

....

16

© Carol Doncaster and Joyce Sweeney 1995.
These pages may not be photocopied.

Complete ☐   Copy ☐   Colour ☐

Here is a big _____.

....

Jill and Tom can _____.

....

© Carol Doncaster and Joyce Sweeney 1995.
These pages may not be photocopied.

Complete ☐   Copy ☐   Colour ☐

The _____ has a cub.

....

Dem is in his _____.

....

Complete ☐   Copy ☐   Colour ☐

Kim has a big _____.

....

Mum has a jar of _____.

....

© Carol Doncaster and Joyce Sweeney 1995.
These pages may not be photocopied.

Find ☐   Write ☐   Colour ☐

nt

bent ✗
tent ✓

....

lt

kilt ☐
felt ☐

....

st

mast ☐
fast ☐

....

ft

soft ☐
raft ☐

....

Complete ☐

1. The man has a red _____.
2. Pam held on to the _____.
3. The _____ is in the van.
4. Ben is at the top of the _____.

Use ☐   fast

Find ☐   Write ☐   Colour ☐

lf
elf ☐
self ☐
....

mp
lamp ☐
camp ☐
....

nd
sand ☐
hand ☐
....

Complete ☐

1. The _____ has a bell on his hat.
2. Nick has cut his _____.
3. Nan has a red _____.

Use ☐   sand

© Carol Doncaster and Joyce Sweeney 1995.
These pages may not be photocopied.

Find ☐   Write ☐   Colour ☐

lk

milk ☐
silk ☐

sk

desk ☐
mask ☐

Complete ☐

1. Dom has lost his _____.
2. The _____ is in the jug.

Use ☐   ask

Find ☐   Write ☐   Colour ☐

nk

pink ☐
sink ☐

nk

bank ☐
sank ☐

nk

junk ☐
bunk ☐

Complete ☐

1. The cups are in the _____.
2. Wilma is on the top _____.
3. Alan has a big _____.

Use ☐   wink

© Carol Doncaster and Joyce Sweeney 1995.
These pages may not be photocopied.

Find ☐   Write ☐   Colour ☐

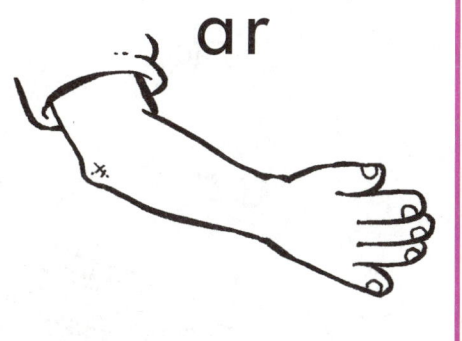

ar

arm ☐
farm ☐

....

ar

car ☐
jar ☐

....

ar

cart ☐
dart ☐

....

Complete ☐

1. Mum went to park the _____.
2. Raj fell and cut his _____.
3. The _____ hit the target.

Use ☐   card

24

© Carol Doncaster and Joyce Sweeney 1995.
These pages may not be photocopied.

Write ☐   Colour ☐

cork	horn	fork
or	or	or

....

Complete ☐

1. Tom dug the garden with a ____.
2. Liz lost the _____ in the bin.
3. Dipti will mend the _____.

Use ☐   cord

Write ☐   Colour ☐

first	girl	bird
ir	ir	ir
....	....	....

Complete ☐

1. If Amar runs fast he will be ___.
2. I met a _____ in the park.
3. A lark is a _____.

Use ☐   dirt

© Carol Doncaster and Joyce Sweeney 1995.
These pages may not be photocopied.

Find ☐   Write ☐   Colour ☐

	b c a r d f s t
	d b z b i r d e
	b g j k i j a r
	v p f o r k m y
	y n h g i r l l
	w f e r n x z

© Carol Doncaster and Joyce Sweeney 1995.
These pages may not be photocopied.

Find ☐ Write ☐

h	f	a	r	m	w	n	s	o	r	t	l
f	o	r	z	k	u	p	a	r	k	g	v
y	b	h	a	r	d	c	j	l	o	r	d

ar

or

s	i	r	p	c	u	r	l	h	e	r	d
o	w	b	u	r	n	x	f	e	r	n	h
k	d	i	r	t	f	h	u	r	t	m	u
e	z	b	b	i	r	d	q	t	e	r	m

ir   **ur**   **er**

© Carol Doncaster and Joyce Sweeney 1995.
These pages may not be photocopied.

Find and write

cork   must   held   task
melt   cart   fist   loft
gift   wink   fond   hint

fork .... mist ....
pink .... mask ....
soft .... mint ....
belt .... pond ....
weld .... rust ....
lift .... dart ....

Draw

a bird in a nest

a girl on a raft